By
Beth Cunningham
& Rebecca Evans
Illustrated by Rebecca Evans

Copyright

Copyright © 2008, Beth Cunningham,
Rebecca Evans & InsideOut Publishing

All rights reserved.
This book, or parts thereof, may not be reproduced
in any form without prior written permission.

Yes I Can!, an InsideOut Empowerment Series for Kids

ISBN: 978-0-9815802-3-4
Library of Congress Control Number: 2008936076

Disclaimer
The services and products offered are exclusively owned by
Inner Element, LLC, all rights reserved. The author(s) of these programs
do not dispense medical advice or prescribe the use of any technique as
a form of treatment for physical or medical problems without the advice
of a physician, either directly or indirectly. The author(s) and publisher
assume no responsibilities for your actions.

InsideOut Publishing is subsidiary of Inner Element, LLC.
www.insideout-publishing.com

Dedication

This book is a creation of love and is dedicated to those who want to truly understand others, inside and out. It is a story with insightful perspective through the world of Kristyn, a young woman with Cerebral Palsy, who chooses to live life without limitations.

Kristyn is a model of inspiration, and it is through her courageous journey in this world, that those of us lucky enough to encounter her have learned many of life's greatest lessons.

She is one of our great teachers and we must pay close attention to the lessons she provides us.

This book is the first in a series dedicated to those with disabilities, our other teachers.

We are paying attention to you.

We are looking at others with our hearts, finally.

Disclaimer for Kids

You have permission to fail.
You have permission to fall down and stay down for awhile.
You have permission to not do your best 100% of the time.
You have permission to have a bad day.
You have permission to feel sad, ugly, lonely and gross.

It takes many steps of falling down to succeed.
It takes many times of starting over to finally "get it done".

You are not broken when you quit. You are closer to succeeding.

Give yourself some room to grow.

You will arrive.

YES YOU CAN!

Introduction

When given the opportunity to teach, I leap. But I must openly admit that I am more of a student than a teacher. I live with a child, my son, who is disabled. And every day I try to pay attention. Every day I try to learn. I know I am fortunate. I get to live with one of life's greatest teachers. He has taught compassion, perseverance, overcoming, love, laughter and perspective. He has taught everyone who comes in contact with him. And I believe he is here for a purpose such as this.

He has taken my hand and led me through his trials and over his mountains with the wisdom of a great guide. I feel indebted to him. I feel lucky.

It is through this realization of my fortune, that I have developed this series, Yes I Can! I feel a moral obligation to share this view with the world, and in doing so, hope to inspire life's great lessons for you as well.

We each have amongst us and within our daily lives, someone who appears unable, but is actually more capable than most we meet.

I chose to direct this series towards children because often children do not see differences in others in a judgmental manner. Children are living lives with eyes wide open and a sense of wonder. I felt this approach could help the grown ups in the world as well. To embrace life with a new pair of eyes. To listen differently. To hear from within. To look and see the abilities in others. To finally learn from the teachers we are each surrounded by and to step up and embrace inclusion.

We are each here for a purpose. Mine, I believe, is to be a student and in turn, share through writing and speaking, the lessons I've absorbed. My son's is to inspire and encourage, reaching everyone with his approachable heart, his lessons as well.

Together, we offer this gift, knowing the intention will impact adults more than children. Knowing that most children will read this and say, "Yes, OF COURSE, I can!"

~ Rebecca Evans

Foreword

Do not focus on limitations. Find your own true spirit and nurture it. Believe in yourself and know that you can accomplish or be anything that you want. Follow your dreams, dream big, and make them worthwhile. Embrace the differences in you and in those around you.

Mission

Yes I Can! is dedicated to empowering people toward their own true potential and goals. We strive to educate by seeking out those who can teach and inspire us the most. We believe that with an open mind and an open heart, all things can be accomplished.

Yes I Can! offers a series of books and products, based on real people in our lives. Visit our website at www.attitudecounts.org to order our next product to inspire you or those you care about.

IDAHO COUNCIL ON DEVELOPMENTAL DISABILITIES

About the Idaho Council on Developmental Disabilities

The MISSION of the Idaho Council on Developmental Disabilities is to promote the capacity of people with developmental disabilities and their families to determine, access and direct the services and/or supports they need to live the lives they choose and to build the communities' ability to support their choices.

The Council is made up of 23 people from all across Idaho. The majority are people with developmental disabilities or parents of children with developmental disabilities. We also have certain state agency members on our Council. We work together to improve services and make sure they are easier for people to get.

The Council does not provide services like therapy. Instead, we work on laws and programs to make life better for people with developmental disabilities in Idaho. Sometimes we provide programs that help people with disabilities and their families become leaders in their communities. We want to see people be successful and to be fully included in their towns and neighborhoods. This means that we work on programs to help people with disabilities have jobs and kids with disabilities go to school with kids without disabilities.

If you would like more information about the Council and the work we do, call 1-800-544-2433 or go to our website at **www.icdd.idaho.gov.**

Community Partnerships of Idaho opened its doors and began serving individuals with disabilities in 1995. Community Partnerships of Idaho's mission is "Creating opportunities for people to learn and achieve their goals". Community Partnerships of Idaho serves children and adults with a variety of disabilities providing a wide range of services in the state of Idaho including mental health counseling and psycho-social rehabilitation, service coordination, residential habilitation, IBI services, developmental therapy services, recreational services and employment services. In addition, Community Partnerships owns Sandcastles Learning Center which is an inclusive and accredited preschool and daycare in Boise, Idaho.

www.cp-of-idaho.com

My Best Friend in the Whole World is...

Kristyn

Her body works a little
differently than mine,
but she can do the same
things as me.

She's smart, she sees,
she hears, she understands,
and most of all...

She is full of
L♡VE

She uses a wheelchair instead of her legs.

She always wins when we RACE.

She uses a picture board for her words.

She is teaching me how to COUNT.

She has a cat named Tessy.

Her cat is very fat.

One of Kristyn's chores is to take care of Tessy.

She takes really good care of Tessy!

Kristyn and I like almost all of the same things...

– playing with dolls
– the color purple

and

–Swimming.

There are times when Kristyn needs some **help**.

When I stay the night, her mom **helps** her into bed.

The one thing that Kristyn does **BETTER** than anyone else is...

...makes me **LAUGH!**

Tips from Kristyn...

- Treat others how you want to be treated.

- Someone in a wheelchair might be shy, so smile and ask them to play.

- Don't be afraid of someone who looks different than you.

- Everyone has the same feelings inside.

- Come talk to me.

- Look at my face.

About Cerebral Palsy

Cerebral Palsy is a neurological disorder that appears in infancy or early childhood which permanently affects the body movement and muscle coordination. It is consistent and does not worsen over time. It is generally caused by trauma in parts of the brain that control muscles. Most people who are diagnosed with Cerebral Palsy are born with it, however it may not be noticed for months or years. Generally, signs of having cerebral palsy are detectable by the age of three. It is possible for a child to have Cerebral Palsy due to brain damage, or a head injury early in life, but this is less common.

There is no cure for cerebral palsy, however treatment such as occupational therapy, speech therapy, and physical therapy may be helpful. Cerebral Palsy has a wide variety of affects and some people may only have a mild impact of walking with a gait, while another person may have his/her mobility, speech and muscle movements impacted.

Research is being done to help determine the causes of Cerebral Palsy.

National Resources

United Cerebral Palsy (UCP)
1660 L Street, NW
Suite 700
Washington, DC 20036
national@ucp.org
http://www.ucp.org
Tel: 202-776-0406 800-USA-5UCP
(872-5827)
Fax: 202-776-0414

March of Dimes Foundation
1275 Mamaroneck Avenue
White Plains, NY 10605
askus@marchofdimes.com
http://www.marchofdimes.com
Tel: 914-428-7100 888-MODIMES
(663-4637)
Fax: 914-428-8203

Children's Neurobiological Solutions (CNS) Foundation
1826 State Street
Santa Barbara, CA 93101
info@cnsfoundation.org
http://www.cnsfoundation.org
Tel: 866-CNS-5580 (267-5580)
805-898-4442

United Cerebral Palsy (UCP) Research & Educational Foundation
1025 Connecticut Avenue
Suite 701
Washington, DC 20036
national@ucp.org
http://www.ucpresearch.org
Tel: 202-496-5060 800-USA-5UCP
(872-5827)
Fax: 202-776-0414

Pathways Awareness Foundation [For Children With Movement Difficulties]
150 N. Michigan Avenue
Suite 2100
Chicago, IL 60601
friends@pathwaysawareness.org
http://www.pathwaysawareness.org
Tel: 312-893-6620 800-955-CHILD (2445)
Fax: 312-893-6621

Easter Seals
230 West Monroe Street
Suite 1800
Chicago, IL 60606-4802
info@easterseals.com
http://www.easterseals.com
Tel: 312-726-6200 800-221-6827
Fax: 312-726-1494

Children's Hemiplegia and Stroke Assoc. (CHASA)
4101 West Green Oaks Blvd., Ste. 305
PMB 149
Arlington, TX 76016
info437@chasa.org
http://www.hemi-kids.org
Tel: 817-492-4325

Pedal with Pete [For Research on Cerebral Palsy]
P.O. Box 274
Kent, OH 44240
petezeid@aol.com
http://www.pedalwithpete.com
Tel: 800-304-PETE (7383)
Fax: 330-673-1240

Local Resources

United Cerebral Palsy of Idaho
5420 W. Franklin
Boise, Idaho 83705
(208) 377-8070 or 1(888)289-3259
info@ucpidaho.org

Community Partnerships of Idaho
3076 N. Five Mile Rd.
Boise, Idaho 83713
(208) 376-6837
www.cp-of-idaho.com

Providing, developmental therapy, employment services, residential habilitation, service coordination, recreational programs, conferences and trainings and counseling.

Idaho Council on Developmental Disabilities
802 W. Bannock Street, Suite 308
Boise, Idaho 83702
Phone: 1-208-334-2178 or 1-800-544-2433
Fax: 1-208-334-3417
info@icdd.idaho.gov

Kristyn

Today, Kristyn lives in Idaho. She was born in December of 1975 in Lafayette General Hospital in Louisiana. The day after she was born, she had a convulsion—like a seizure and was unable to breathe for about 10 minutes. Her body was unable to get enough oxygen into its body tissues and this caused damage to her brain.

Her birth parents gave her up for adoption two weeks later. She moved around foster homes until the age of eight. Then she moved to Idaho and was adopted.

Even though she has CP, she does not have an attitude like someone with limitations. She knows she can do anything she sets her mind to. For example, she has gone camping and white water rafting. On her 26th birthday, she even went sky diving. Her motto at the end of every email is "if there's a will, there's a way", and she lives the motto every day, inspiring the rest of us with far more limitations than her.

Kristyn and her cat, Tessy

Beth Cunningham

Beth Cunningham began learning about and meeting people with disabilities at a very young age due to her parents who worked in this field. Beth obtained a Bachelor's Degree in Psychology from the University of Tennessee and then moved to Colorado to pursue a job as a white water raft guide.

She returned to school in Colorado and obtained a Master's Degree in Rehabilitation Counseling and Vocational Evaluation from the University of Northern Colorado. Beth has been working in the disability field since 1993 and is currently the director of Employment Services for Community Partnerships of Idaho. Beth and her department are committed to assisting individuals with disabilities to obtain gainful employment through vocational evaluation, counseling and placement services. Beth believes that employment is one key aspect in independence. Beth has a passion to assist people of all abilities to achieve their goals and to become independent.

Beth lives in Boise Idaho with her two young daughters, Gracie and Ella and her husband Troy. She feels that education along with experiences at a young age is very important for kids to learn and to truly appreciate and value diversity.

Rebecca Evans

Rebecca Evans is a motivational speaker, author and empowerment coach. She founded Inner Element as a way to combine her experiences as a woman in the military, mom and world class athlete into an organization that provides effective life breakthrough strategies. Her core philosophy, "fitness from the inside out" resounds for men and women of all ages. As a frequent columnist, radio show host and frequent television guest, she shares her empowerment techniques with thousands of individuals weekly. Her accomplishments as a business woman have landed her as Idaho Business Review's *"Idaho Women of the Year"* honors, the National Association of Women Business Owners *Business Women of the Year* honors, and Boise State University's *"Women Making History in Idaho"*. She is a former *Girls on the Run* program director, Mrs. Idaho International 2004 and a decorated Gulf War veteran. She is the author of *The Art of Self Discovery, Inner Fitness for Celebrating Your Life, Inner Fitness for Girls* and *Inner Fitness for Empowerment* and lives in Idaho with her husband and three children.